# DON'T GIVE UP
## with Lee the Fox

Illustrated by
**JANAE BARGER**

Written by
**DARCI DAVIDSON**

Printed in the United States of America

ISBN: 978-1-7341819-1-3

Dedicated to my Mom, Sharon, who imparted to me a love for brimmed hats, stacks of books, coffee house tunes, old broncos & everything linen. She also, through her life's example, taught me to not give up even when it gets really hard—and so I teach mine!

And to

All of my children and the children who read this, based on a true story, story. You are stronger than you know, and when you reach the end of your strength (at times you will), then remember you have a big God, who's big enough for it ALL.

Love, Darci

I waited and waited for just the right one.
They tried try to sell me here and there,
but no one seemed to have an interest,
like no one cared.

Then one day it finally happened. A boy named Jett bought me with his birthday money. He brought me home, as happy as could be, and he gave me his middle name, "Lee."

He tied me to a leash and took me for walks.
I'm a "domesticated" silver pearl fox.

"Domesticated" to be a pet, but it didn't take long for Jett to figure out I was still wild and wanted to roam about.

He made me a den and gave me chew toys. This house was full of rambunctious girls and boys!

They would come in and out to play.
Jett even took a nap with me one day.

I had plenty to eat and plenty of fresh water. He loved me and cared for me like no other.

But I have a lot of energy and senses that are very strong. I can smell things from a half mile long!

I got curious one day and decided
to go out to play. So I dug and dug
and I dug down deep.
I kept digging while everyone was asleep.

I crawled out of the hole I made.
I had so much energy I just ran and played!
It was so much fun to be myself and to be
free—it really wasn't easy to tame me.

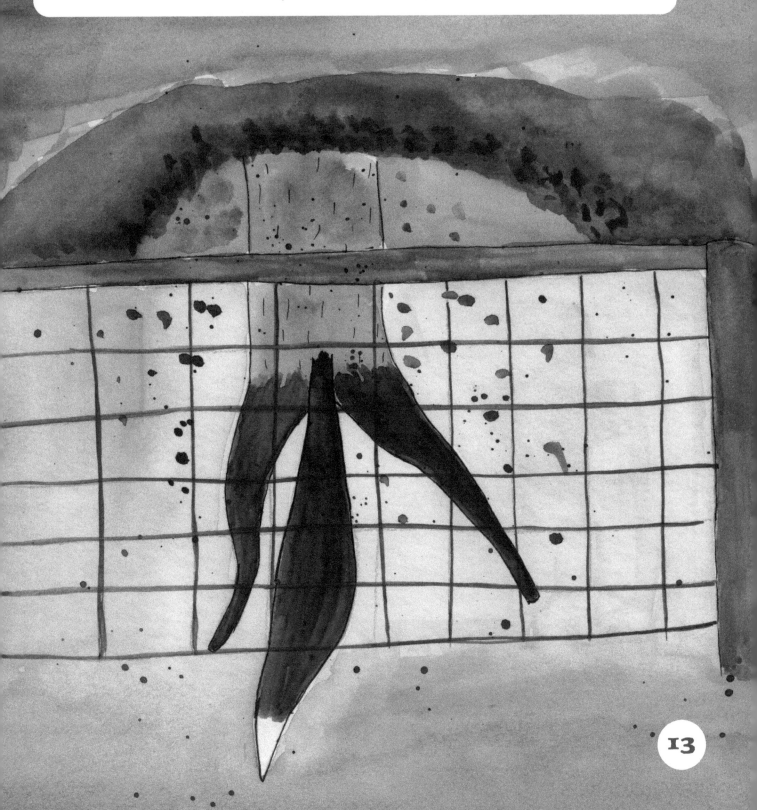

I found SO many fun
things along the way.

14

I got into some trouble, too,
but being free and running wild
was what I was made to do!

15

In the morning, Jett saw the hole
I had dug and that I was gone.

He looked and looked and kept
looking for me everywhere.

He yelled for me and prayed.
Then he realized I was gone and
there was nothing more to do.
Jett was feeling so blue.

I didn't know
because I was out
to explore and play,
but Jett was sad
for many days.

Then he realized I wasn't coming back. I was free, as free as a hawk!

But Jett was determined to tame a fox, so he used his energy to save more money, working as hard as a bee making honey.

22

He cleaned the pen and got it ready,
knowing soon he'd have another buddy.
He made a few changes to the pen,
determined to keep a wild fox in.

You know, sometimes things don't
work out the way we want.
But don't give up! Keep your mind
on God and not on your "luck."

With faith and this perspective, better days are sure to be around the corner and when they come you'll be wiser and stronger.

Keep believing, don't quit and work hard at what you have to do! You'll be amazed at what God will do through YOU!

At times it may get hard—much harder than you thought, but if it's right, it's worth the fight.

Fight the good fight of faith.
1 Timothy 6:12

# Author

Darci has always had a love for words written in a way to make people think or feel something positive and lasting. Poetry found a special place in in her heart in high school, when she lost her older brother to an accident and a friend gave her a poem that helped her put language to the way she felt at the time. Poetry didn't take away the questions or pain, but helped her understand the feelings were normal and that others have been there, too, and made it through. Although she spent a lot of time traveling, she kept her roots in her childhood rural town in Ohio, where she lives with her husband and six children. Most days she can be found in the kitchen preparing food for the many people God brings to sit around her table, tending to the backyard homestead or at her co-owned health food store & farm to table restaurant. Her passion is Jesus and to encourage others who are on this faith journey with her. She loves to write rhymes, cultivating words and stories that speak to both the reader and the listener, in a simple, relatable, yet powerful way! She enjoys creating opportunities for people to disconnect from their busy lives, curl up somewhere for a few minutes and connect through a story. She is also the author of the children's book "But for Now, Stay Here."

# Illustrator

Ever since Janae was a child, she couldn't pick just one favorite color—all colors were her favorite. In fact, when she was asked her favorite color the first day of school, panic filled her mind as they went around the room to share that simple "ice breaker." All she could think to say was "pink" as they went around the classroom. After all, she was a girly girl so it only made sense. Her teacher playfully responded, "Pink isn't a color... It's a shade." Little did she know, she'd carry that funny, yet intimidating, moment with her for the rest of her life. That same high school art teacher saw a light in her that needed to shine as Janae spent the rest of her high school career finding a love for watercolors and ink. In her adult years she has devoted her passion to caring for children. That meant a lot of reading and a lot of crafts! But truthfully, crafts were not her thing. She felt her happiest when painting murals on the windows in the daycare, and getting messy on hand painting days. Painting was her passion! She then found herself in a small business helping with color schemes and playing with dyes. Stepping stone after stepping stone and with immense support from her husband, Derek, she finally felt at home while illustrating. Finding bright colors that kids can relate to and painting the messiness of dirt and neutral color schemes to create a fun space on each page only made sense. To be blossoming into what God planted in her heart on that first day of art class and to reach the hearts of little ones, she hopes to always inspire children to do what God created them for. The gifts and talents planted in her were not only for her own use, but for the glory of God and to reach others through her for Him. So, whatever God has planted in you, remember to use it for God's goodness. (2 Corinthians 9:12)

Printed in the USA
CPSIA information can be obtained
at www.ICGtesting.com
LVHW061228161123
763684LV00002B/8